Leading While Green

How Emerging Leaders Can Ripen Into Effective Leaders

by

Pierre Quinn

Lisa,
Thanks so much for your courage & leadership!

For Bill, Barb, & Ashleigh

ACKNOWLEDGEMENTS

Thanks to everyone who supported this book project. Thanks to my wife Coleen and my daughters Briana and Ella for letting me stay cooped up in my room for hours while working on the manuscript. Thanks to my mentor and friend Andre Anderson for your invaluable insights for the years. Thanks to my lead editor Josh Raab who helped me say what I was trying to say in a much better way. Thanks to my Leading While Green launch team for your support and for sharing your leadership journey with me and with each other.

"A man's gift makes room for him and brings him before great men."

-Proverbs 18:16

Contents

Acknowledgements	iv
Introduction	vii
Lesson 1: It's Not Easy Being Green	1
Lesson 2: How You Got Picked	10
Lesson 3: The Power Of Myths	20
Lesson 4: The Mantle Of Leadership	30
Lesson 5: Too Far Too Fast	39
Lesson 6: The Leader's Square	49
Lesson 7: The Opportunity of a Lifetime	60
Lesson 8: How To Win Over Most of Your Critics	68
Lesson 9: The Benefits of Getting Things Wrong	78
Lesson 10: Taking Notes On The Journey	88
Lesson 11: Team Leadership For Green Leaders	96
Lesson 12: Learning To Hang On	109
About The Author	118

Introduction

Do any of these phrases sound familiar?

You're still wet behind the ears.

You still need training wheels.

You'll get the hang of it.

You need someone to hold your hand.

You're too green.

The real world doesn't look favorably upon beginners. Young leaders who are given the opportunity to excel are, more often than not, simultaneously reminded by the same ol' cynics just how young and inexperienced they are; just how large of a road they have ahead of them.

If you can relate to this experience in any way then you are exactly the person I had in mind while writing this book

With more than a decade of experience teaching leadership principles to college students, I've helped scores of young adults discover their leadership potential and begin their journey toward powerful and confident leadership. The tools I share in this book have helped teachers, entrepreneurs, ministry leaders, marketing directors, and business coaches navigate their journeys from green to experienced.

I promise that as you read Leading While Green you will discover that, at this very moment, you have all of the skills you need to become the leader you were meant to be.

Don't be just another emerging leader with tremendous potential, but who never lives up to it. Don't be the one who lets fears and naysayers keep you from growing, be the kind of leader who has earned the admiration of your peers and the respect of your elders.

Leadership is messy. This book may come in a nice, tidy package, but your leadership journey will not. There will be twists and turns. You'll experience mud pits and thorn bushes. If it wasn't tough then you wouldn't appreciate the privilege of leading.

If you persevere, you will have more than the basic possibility of success, you'll have the legitimate probability.

I wish you all the best on your leadership journey.

Lesson 1: It's Not Easy Being Green

In December 2008, Sesame Street posted a video on their YouTube channel that quickly received over 7 million views. Just under two minutes long, the video features Kermit the frog singing his away his troubles. The name of the song is "It's Not Easy Being Green."

For the first half of the song, Kermit sings about the struggles that come with being green. He sings about wanting to be different. He sings about all the things that overwhelm him about his color and halfway through the song, you can't help but sympathize with Kermit. Why should being green make his life so difficult? As the tempo shifts, Kermit reminds himself of all the good things associated with the color green. He sings of the potential of green things to be big, important, or tall. At the end of the song, he reaches a point of resolution. If green is what he is, then he's okay with being green.

Like Kermit, you've probably wrestled with what it means to be green. Now I know green has some positive connotations. When we think of green, we can think of recycling or saving the trees or conservation. We can think of newness, freshness or nature. However, when it comes to leadership, the connotation is negative: it means you're inexperienced.

What does it mean to be a green leader?

When I was a child, out for a grocery run with my mom, she always told me to stay away from the green bananas. Why? "The greener the bunch, the longer you'll have to wait before getting to eat them," she'd say. Well, the same goes for leaders, when people look at you, they think you're not ready, not ripe, not mature enough to lead effectively. The purpose of this book is to help you embrace the real possibility of leading effectively while continuing to ripen as a leader.

At 30-years-old, I moved to Kentucky and was given the incredible responsibility of being the leader of a small congregation. The average age of senior pastors in the United States is 50-years-old. My new congregation was used to having a more seasoned leader at the helm and they made sure to remind me of this on several occasions.

By the time I moved to Kentucky, I had already taught college courses for several years, spoken across the country, and traveled around the world. These accomplishments meant nothing to my congregation. All they saw was a young kid, fresh out of seminary in need of their help as he learned how to ride the bike of ministry without any training wheels. They had doubts about my maturity, which beget doubts about my competency, which resulted in their not trusting my leadership. They didn't feel I was ripe enough. After being formally introduced to the congregation and preaching for the worship, a few of the members walked up to me and said some things that, thinking back, I should have expected to hear.

One lady, who seemed well intentioned, asked me how old I was. I responded to her that I was 30 and she chuckled and shook her head a little bit as she bemoaned, "I have grandkids who are your age." At that point I felt like someone had stuck a pin in my balloon. Then she said, "Don't worry, you might not know much now, but by the time we're done with you, you'll have been taught everything that you need to know." Another member of the congregation walked up to me and said, "Man, you sure do look young."

I was starting to feel bad. I wanted to grab a microphone and read my résumé, but who would have cared? The members saw what they wanted to see. You'll come across this in your endeavors at every turn: when people look at you they see what they want to see.

Retired four-star general and former Secretary of State, Colin Powell, identifies trust as a key quality of effective leadership. He defines leadership as “creating conditions of trust in organizations”. My own working definition is “encouraging people to step in the direction of what they have the potential to become.” In Powell’s definition, trust is explicit. According to mine, it is implied. In both cases, outcomes are dependent upon people believing in you strongly enough to let you lead them. Experiencing success as young leader can be difficult as you strive to develop the confidence in yourself and gain the trust of the people you are called to lead. When people trust you, they allow you to help them move forward.

Movement requires trust. Gaining that trust takes time.

I wonder how long it took Dr. Martin Luther King Jr. to build trust with others who were fighting for civil rights? Dr. King was selected to be president of the newly formed Montgomery Improvement Association. What was his first major task? Leading the Montgomery Bus Boycott. I wonder how many people thought he was too green, at 26-years old, for this role.

When Murray Schumach wrote King's obituary, which appeared in the New York Times, he noted that King's newness actually helped him get the job. He hadn't been around long enough to develop enemies among those he was to lead. King went on to be the face of the civil rights movement and one of the most influential leaders in American history. He was assassinated at the age of 39, but his efforts continued to be heralded today.

I wonder how long it took Julie Smolyanksy to build trust? Julie's father, Michael, a Russian immigrant in Chicago, started Lifeway Foods in 1986. The business grew into a multimillion-dollar industry. Michael tragically died from a heart attack in 2002, leaving his daughter to take over the business.

At the time, she was only 27. An ABC News report quoted Julie as saying, “right after my father died, people said to my face, ‘no way a 27-year-old could run a publicly traded company.” Under Julie’s leadership Lifeway Foods grew from a 12-million dollar company to a 75-million dollar company. In 2014, Julie was listed as one of Fortune Magazine’s Top 40 under 40.

Dr. King learned how to lead well.

Julie Smolyanksy learned how to lead well.

You can learn to learn well if you put the effort in.

The Wrap Up

Once you develop confidence in your abilities and effectively earn the trust of your followers, leadership moves from being just possible to being probable. If a frog puppet can come to terms with being green, then there's hope for you and me.

Key Questions To Ripening Well:

1. Review some of the challenges you've faced as a young leader. In what areas do you have doubts about your own ability to lead? In what areas do you have confidence in your ability to lead?

2. Describe an experience of someone making reference to your age in relationship to your leadership role. How did you respond?

Lesson 2: How You Got Picked

Without a list, I'm a terrible grocery shopper.

My wife cringes each time I have to pick up something from the store without her. That's why she sends me with a list. If I stick to the list I'm safe. With the list I don't spend a lot of time inspecting, comparing or analyzing. I grab what's needed and move on. When my wife goes to the grocery store, it's a totally different experience. There's a tremendous amount of analysis, comparison and inspection that takes place, especially when it comes to picking fruit.

When I pick bananas I just grab the ones that aren't too green. That's pretty much the beginning and ending of my thought process. My wife's set of criteria is a bit more extensive. She scrutinizes not only the color but the size, the number in the bunch, and the proximity to other bananas. For my wife, there are several questions that need to be answered before a bunch of bananas can be admitted into her cart.

Have you ever thought about how you ended up where you are? Let's take your current role for example. Are you a departmental director, are you a dean, are you the president of a student group or a campus club, are you a senior pastor, are you a director of sales, are you an athletic coordinator?

When was the last time you asked yourself why they picked you?

If you haven't yet, you should. Regardless of your responsibility, you didn't get there by accident. And there wasn't just one thing that made them pick you, it was a combination of factors. They considered your experiences, attributes, and relationships. Understanding the each of these factors is vital to understanding what qualifies you to lead.

Your Experiences

What's listed on your resume under the experience section? You might not have previous experience directly related to your current role, but you have definitely had experiences that you learned from. Maybe you worked for a company for a few years before being granted a leadership role. What happened in those years before you were given your current responsibilities? What scenarios allowed you to acquire some of the skills that are necessary for you to lead? By reviewing your experiences you'll find that even some of the minor roles and responsibilities have taught you useful lessons about leadership. One summer I worked with a group of other pastors to pitch pole tents for a children's camp. For a week we traded sermons for sledgehammers. Our foreman was an older pastor who was known for traveling the country setting up tents for tent revivals. One day while working the foreman called for a break and told us to grab some water. A few of the guys kept working because they wanted to get the job finished faster. The rest of us sat with the foreman to chat. Looking out at the guys who didn't take a break he said, "I learned a long time ago to watch the foreman. When he takes a break you take a break. When he works you work. The foreman knows best."

This group was used to leading churches but not taking orders. These leaders were now being asked to follow. That experience taught me that good leadership means having an ability to follow.

Your Attributes

Brian Tracy knows about leadership. A one-time leader of a $265 million dollar development company Tracy now works for himself as an international speaker and seminar leader. His company, Brian Tracy International, specialized in the training and development of organizations.

In a YouTube video Brian Tracy shares what he believes to be the seven essential qualities of all great leaders. Those qualities are vision, courage, integrity, humility, strategic planning, the ability to achieve results, and the willingness to focus on strengths of your people and the organization.

To have been given a leadership position means that you have demonstrated some combination of these attributes.

Your Relationships

Simply holding on to what you know is not enough to get your far. It's who you know and who knows you that makes all the difference.

"One of the challenges in networking is everybody thinks it's making cold calls to strangers. Actually, it's the people who already have strong trust relationships with you, who know you're dedicated, smart, a team player, who can help you."

-Reid Hoffman

Several years ago I served as a member of a search committee that was looking for a senior development officer. As we were reviewing resumes, we would periodically make calls to check references. For internal applicants, the search committee took the conversation one step further. We went around the table asking each other what we knew and how we felt about the applicant. Many times your placement as a leader is largely determined by your pre-existing relationship to someone else. That doesn't mean you should kiss up to people or move unethically, but you need to understand the power of relationships, and how both positive and negative experiences can come back to help or hinder you.

How To Increase Your Chances Of Getting Picked Again

1. Review Your Story

We claim to know ourselves, but do we really know our story? It is important for all leaders to review their leadership journey. Consider making a leadership timeline of your major life and professional experiences. What has each one of those major life milestones done to your professional life and taught you about yourself? Review those experiences and glean insight from them as the days, weeks, months and years go by.

2. Refine Your Attributes

How well do you demonstrate the attributes listed by Brian Tracy? If you have a perfect score in all of those areas, you're either on a TV show, in a movie, or playing a video game. No one in real life is perfect in every area. There is always room for improvement. What are the steps you can take to firm up on your weak spots?

3. Tend To Your Relationships

We need to nurture our relationships. As a leader, your network should grow, not shrink. Strong relationships are nurtured relationships. We all have people who are important to us, who have mentored us, and who have helped us identify and promote our leadership qualities. It's always good to continue checking in with those people. A quick phone call or a meet up over a meal is a great way to stay connected.

The Wrap Up

You were picked to be a leader because you have had experiences that have helped unearth your potential. You were picked because you've demonstrated at least one of the attributes that characterize great leadership. You were picked because someone recognized your value.

Keys Questions To Ripening Well:

1. Create a leadership timeline. Identify the key life experiences that have helped shape you into a leader. What are some of the lessons you've learned from each of those experiences?

2. Which of the key qualities of leadership listed by Brian Tracy do you need to further refine the most?

3. Set up a lunch meeting with those who selected you for your current leadership role. Ask them what led them to select you for your position.

Lesson 3: The Power Of Myths

Parson Weems was a wonderful storyteller.

Born Mason Locke Weems, Weems was a minister, book agent, and author. Though he died in 1825 ,the world still feels the impact of his stories. In 1806, Weems published his book "The Life and Memorable Actions of George Washington." In the book, Weems shares a story about a young George Washington admitting to his father that chopped down a cherry tree. Instead of punishing the young George, who had just famously declared that he couldn't tell a lie, his father admonished him for telling the truth.

There's just one problem with this age-old story: it never really happened. The story is a product of Parson's imagination, it's nothing more than myth. A myth is a traditional or legendary story without a determinable basis of fact or a natural explanation.

There's just something about myths that appeals to us. Consider these three famous ones.

Eve Ate An Apple

In this classic story of the first man and the first woman, it is often noted that Eve was tempted by a snake to eat an apple. Artistic interpretations over the years always tell us it was an apple. In the actual Biblical account of this story, no specific fruit is mentioned.

Bacon and Eggs are the All-American Breakfast

In the 1920s, the Beech-Nut Packing Company manufactured a whole host of food items including jam, peanut butter, biscuits, coffee, mustard, and pork. While they were embarking on a PR campaign, they discovered that Americans traditionally ate a light breakfast consisting most times of coffee and a small Danish or a piece of fruit.

So what happened?

Beech-Nut found a doctor who agreed that it would have been better for Americans to eat a heavier breakfast. Beech-Nut then convinced the doctor to write to 5,000 other doctors and ask them to agree on the need for Americans to eat a heartier breakfast.

Many of these 5,000 doctors suggested publicly that bacon and eggs should become part of the morning diet for the average American. With that recommendation plastered on newspaper front pages around the country, the sales of bacon and other pork products increased wildly, leading to great dividends for the Beech-Nut Packing Company. Thus the All-American breakfast was born.

Bananas Grow on Trees

The banana plant is not a tree. It's actually the world's largest perennial herb. Bananas are technically berries that don't produce seeds. The root systems of a banana plant grow large and aboveground. These roots are often mistaken as tree trunks, but they don’t contain any woody tissue. Without woody tissue the banana plant cannot be categorizes as a tree.

You Probably Believe A Myth About Yourself

There is a popular myth about leadership: previous experience always leads to instant credibility.

Now, this may be true for established leaders, but isn't usually the case for emerging leaders. Review your leadership timeline again. What are some of your previous experiences? Maybe you were class president. Maybe you were a project leader. Maybe you interned at a Fortune 500 company. Maybe you grew up in a family business or you studied overseas. Maybe you were the captain of your college baseball team, or maybe you were an MBA graduate. These opportunities have lead to experiences but those experiences don’t always translate to credibility. If you have been given the opportunity to lead at this stage, you have been given what John Maxwell described as positional leadership.

Several years ago there was a popular FedEx commercial about a guy on his first day at the job. As he's sitting at his desk, a woman walks up to him and says, "I know this is your first day, can you give us a hand with something?" He says, "Sure, no problem." The lady walks him to the shipping room and says, "We need you to help us get this shipping done and we got to get this stuff out today." The guy says, "I don't do shipping." She says, "Oh, it's really easy. We use FedEx and it makes shipping our packages really easy." He says, "You don't understand. I have an MBA." She says, "Oh, you have an MBA. Well, then I better show you how we do this."

Well, if you didn't get the joke, the new employee was suggesting that his experienced as an MBA student instantly made him more credible, granted him more privilege, and allowed him to avoid what he deemed a menial task of shipping. It doesn't...Just because you graduated at the top of your class, led an overseas study tour, or interned on Capitol Hill, doesn't automatically translate into leverage or trust. You have only positional leadership. A positional leader is followed simply because of their position. People listen to you because you are categorically in charge and they respect the position, not because they trust you.

Believing the myth that your previous experience leads to instant credibility may cause you to experience several leadership temptations.

Temptation #1: Thinking You Know More Than You Do

Your leadership timeline may have revealed several experiences that led to your current opportunity, but here's the truth: you don't know as much as you think you do. Take the humble road, and listen before you speak. Ask before you suggest, and think before you act.

Temptation #2: Ignoring the Concerns of Those You're leading

Your team members are concerned about your youth. They're concerned about your inexperience. They have questions about your competence. A mistake young leaders tend to make is avoiding these concerns by simply ignoring them.

Temptation #3: Bulldozing Obstacles

This is when a leader tries to use anger, fear, intimidation, or manipulation to achieve progress. Having to remind someone that you're in charge is often evidence of a leadership failure. In this way, positional leadership comes with limited leverage.

Temptation #4: Avoiding Decision Making

There is a disease young leaders can contract called decision paralysis. Decision paralysis is being so afraid to make the wrong decision that you don't make any decision at all. When I started early on as a ministry leader, I called my mentor on a weekly basis with questions, concerns, and challenges I was facing. At the end of each conversation, he would say, "well, you are the leader. You have to make a decision. I can give you all the advice and support you need, but I can't make decisions for you."

The Wrap Up

We all are tempted. The trouble begins when we give into the temptations. Avoiding leadership temptations will increase your capacity and longevity as a leader.

Keys Questions To Ripening Well:

1. Make a list of all the concerns that others may have about your ability to lead. How many items on the list are legitimate concerns? Which ones are you willing to address?

2. Identify areas in which you could use some assistance but haven't asked for it. Setup meetings this week to ask for the assistance you need.

3. In what areas are you avoiding your responsibility to make a decision? What is keeping you from taking the necessary steps? How will you overcome these obstacles?

Lesson 4: The Mantle Of Leadership

There is an ancient Hebrew story about a well-known prophet and his apprentice, a young farmer.

This notable spiritual leader appears on the scene and initially speaks no words to the young farmer. He only executes a simple gesture. This gesture inspires the young farmer to ask the prophet for the opportunity to say goodbye to his family. The prophet grants the request, and the farmer feasts with his family before setting off on a life-changing adventure as the prophet's apprentice.

What's key to the story is the fact that the prophet never formally asked the young farmer to follow him. He simply made a symbolic gesture that conveyed the request without words.

What was the single action that meant so much?

In the story, we are told that prophet placed his mantle on the young farmer. In a practical sense, a mantle is a piece cloth used as a head wrap or placed around the shoulders or waist, but symbolically, when we speak of passing the mantle, we mean that the prophet was preparing to hand over his leadership to the young farmer.

What's crazy about this whole story is that it almost didn't happen.

The prophet had previously battled depression, like all leaders do sooner or later. One moment the prophet experienced success in the royal court as he was challenging the character and actions of the king. The next morning, he was running for his life because of a threat that came from the king's wife. If you haven't yet, you will experience all the emotions that come with the peaks and valleys of leadership.

Finding seclusion in a cave, the ancient narrative tells us, God visited the prophet. The prophet wrapped his mantle around his head and left the cave to have a conversation with God. God's instructions were clear, if the prophet didn't move forward, a young farmer wouldn't grow into his destiny. The leadership of this young farmer was dependent upon the famous prophet embracing the disappointments of his calling. Listening to the voice of God made the prophet set out to meet the young farmer. Near the end of the prophet's life, another symbolic action takes place as his life on Earth is ending, the prophet drops his mantle to ground.

For some time the farmer had followed right behind the prophet, tracing his actions and studying his leadership, but now the leadership of this prophet has come to an end. The young farmer grabs the mantle and wraps it around himself and begins to take new footsteps. Previously, he walked as a farmer and as an apprentice, now he's walking as the new spiritual leader, now he's walking as a prophet.

But what did he do by picking up the mantle?

In a practical sense, the young farmer picked up the piece of cloth he had seen wrapped around the prophet's body numerous times. In a symbolic sense, he did much more than that. By picking up the mantle, the young farmer picked up the rights, privileges, and perks of leadership that the prophet had enjoyed. But, by picking up the mantle, the young farmer also picked up the responsibilities, and the burden of leadership that the prophet had carried. By saying "yes" to being a leader, this former farmer was saying yes to both the rights and responsibilities of leadership.

Wise leaders do not separate the rights of leadership from the responsibilities of leadership.

Our job descriptions may call for us to look out for others but we might have bought into the idea of only looking out for ourselves.

Leaders who are ripening well understand that leading is less above sitting back and watching and more about getting up and setting an example.

A mantle is an important role or responsibility that passes from one person to another. The most significant part of wearing the mantle as a leader is looking after people. When I taught my first college course, I was focused, mainly in the beginning, on imparting my knowledge to my students. I thought that the privilege of being in charge was the most important thing. What I eventually learned was that equally important to teaching the class and sharing the knowledge was helping the students navigate this stage of their lives. Being in charge of the class was one of the perks. Taking care of the students was the responsibility.

Consider those things you get to do that no one does. Consider the meetings that sit in on, the accounts you have access to, and the flexibility you wield. How you are using or abusing these as a leader?

Are you helping those under your leadership take steps in the right direction?

The Wrap Up

Leaders who ripen well understand that you can't be so committed to your position that you neglect your people. Good leaders have a healthy balance between the rights and responsibilities of leadership.

Keys Questions To Ripening Well:

1. Describe your experience dealing with the peaks and valleys of leadership.

2. What are some of the privileges afforded to you by your current leadership role?

3. What are some of the responsibilities of leadership that you are having a difficult time accepting or you've been avoiding?

Lesson 5: Too Far Too Fast

Boarding school life is unique.

I graduated from high school, with less than a hundred students, in a small country town in the middle of nowhere. The founders built the school in a place where students could learn with minimal distractions. There isn't much to do in the middle of nowhere, but amazingly some students still found ways to get into trouble.

Our Sundays at school were about pickup basketball. We would play in an old gym built without air-conditioning affectionately named the "hotbox." We didn't need food and we didn't need breaks. Most of the games were great, but every now and then a game would take turn for the worst.

The cause? Someone's girlfriend dropped by the gym to say hi.

When the girlfriends showed up pride kicked in and bravado ensued. Strangely enough, you probably act the same way today when you're trying to impress someone.

Good players know that you have to let the game come to you. That idea flies out the window when you're trying to look good in front of your girl. Instead of playing with focus, the guys would start talking too much, taking too many shots, and trying to be too fancy. They would do too much, go too far, and move too fast. And when you move too far and too fast eventually the fun dies.

How long did it take you to recover from the last time you moved too far and too fast?

Scott Livengood learned this later in life.

You've have probably never heard of Scott Livengood, but you're probably aware of the company he used to work for. Scott is the former CEO of Krispy Kreme Doughnuts, and he chose to retire after 28-years with the company. When you are a senior executive working for a major company and things don't work out, there are options. You either choose to step down or deal with the embarrassment of a public firing.

So what was the problem?

Krispy Kreme had built an impressive brand over the years. In the year 2000, Livengood was brought in to help continue building the brand. Under his direction, the company developed an aggressive expansion plan and built several new stores. With the building of new stores and extending the sale of their products to gas stations and grocery stores they eventually saturated their own market. Stores moved into competition with each other and overall profits decreased. They expanded way too fast in order to keep up with the demands for their doughnuts. As the company suffered, Livengood fell out of favor with the board. The once impeccable Krispy Kreme brand had been tarnished and Livengood had to go.

That's what can happen when you move too far too fast.

Julie Wainwright learned this too.

In 1999, Julie Wainwright took over as the CEO of Pets.com. She joined a team of veteran executives intent on making their company a major player in the pet supplies industry. Before Pets.com launched, they had established an amazing team who thought they had a great plan. In addition, they secured a partnership with Amazon.com to help ensure the backing they needed to stand out against the competition. How could the right team with the right experience and the right backing ever fail?

The answer is in the pace.

Pets.com had both an aggressive marketing strategy and an aggressive price structure. They wanted to build their business so incredibly fast that the competition wouldn't be able to keep up and they were willing to do this no matter the cost. What was the result of all that injection of resources in such a short amount of time? In 2000, pets.com sold the domain name to one of its rivals PetSmart.com. Low interest in their offerings and slim profit margins just didn't allow them to stay viable.

That's what can happen when you move too far too fast.

And finally, Moses learned this too.

Moses was born into the Hebrew depression at time when the Egyptians' genocide targeting male Hebrew children was in full swing. In desperation, his mother placed him in a tar-covered basket and sent him floating downriver with the hopes of him being saved by some caring individual. That caring individual turned out to be Pharaoh's daughter. In a peculiar twist of events, Moses did get to grow up at home with his family, but went on to live in Egypt during his formative years. His Hebrew heritage and Egyptian training lead to a tremendous amount of leadership potential. Some even argue that he would have probably made a great pharaoh. One day, Moses saw an Egyptian beating a Hebrew slave. Although this was a scene he knew all too well, this time it struck a chord in Moses. He snapped. Moses killed the Egyptian and buried him in the sand. Moses would eventually lead the children of Israel but not at this time and not like this. As a result of this misstep he had to flee for his own life.

That's what can happen when you move too far too fast.

It's all about the pace.

One of Aesop's most famous fables is The Tortoise and the Hare. Check out the fable in its entirety.

The Hare was once boasting of his speed before the other animals. "I have never yet been beaten," said he, "when I put forth my full speed. I challenge any one here to race with me."

The Tortoise said quietly, "I accept your challenge."

"That is a good joke," said the Hare; "I could dance round you all the way."

"Keep your boasting till you've won," answered the Tortoise. "Shall we race?"

So a course was fixed and a start was made. The Hare darted almost out of sight at once, but soon stopped and, to show his contempt for the Tortoise, lay down to have a nap. The Tortoise plodded on and plodded on, and when the Hare awoke from his nap, he saw the Tortoise just near the winning post and could not run up in time to save the race.

Then the Tortoise said: "Slow but steady progress wins the race."

If you put these two animals side-by-side and wagered ask which one would win, most people would pick the hare. It seems like a no-brainer: the hare should win every time. The hare is designed to run. The hare is faster. The hare has a clear advantage.

Why does the tortoise win?

As the hare zipped out ahead, his overconfidence in his abilities moved him to take a nap in the middle of a race! Had the hare maintained the right pace we wouldn't have a lesson to learn from this story. But, outmatched in nearly every way except brains, the tortoise maintained a steady pace and it was this pace that led him to surpass the hare.

As a leader, you are a pacesetter. The question is are you setting the right pace?

The CEO of Krispy Kreme, the CEO of Pets.com and Moses all made major mistakes when they tried to move things too far and too fast. Your efforts must have a steady pace in the right direction. Remember, leadership is about helping people take steps in the direction of their potential. But, your ability to execute this is dependent upon your pace, and as a leader you have to achieve a pace you can reasonably sustain.

Keys Questions To Ripening Well:

1. Good leaders set a good pace to accomplishing goals in their organization. What are some of the goals that you need to accomplish?

2. Are you currently moving at a reasonable pace? In what areas do you need to speed up or slow down?

Lesson 6: The Leader's Square

For the German Insurance Division (GDV), banana boxes are a big deal.

The GDV has specific regulations regarding the transport of bananas. This organization understands that in order for bananas to make it safely to their intended destinations, they need to be handled properly. The regulations established by the GDV include specifics regarding the packaging materials, the size of the packaging, and its design.

Bananas transported in the right boxes have a strong likelihood of making it to their intended destination in an acceptable condition. Imagine attempting to transport a bunch of bananas without the right boxes. The end result would most likely be visually unappealing and possibly inedible bananas. Banana boxes were developed so that bananas can make it safely to where they need to go. For that to happen the bananas need to stay inside the box.

Let's shift our concept from a box to a square and let's call it The Leader's Square. Inside the square is the sum total of your ability to lead. The square is how you will grow, how you will learn, how you will be protected. You'll be much safer along your leadership journey if you learn to stay inside the square. So what makes up your leader square?

There are four components to the leader square:

BEING MENTORED	MENTORING SOMEONE
CONNECTING WITH PEERS	BEING SUPPORTED

Being Mentored

I interviewed leadership architect, change strategist, and author of Leadership Pain, Dr. Sam Chand about his leadership journey. Dr. Chand shared that one of his biggest mistakes was not connecting with his mentors earlier in his leadership journey.

With origins in Greek mythology, the term mentor is developed to mean a trusted advisor or counselor. Think about who your ideal mentor might be. As a speaker, I would love to be mentored by Les Brown or John Maxwell. As an educator, I would love to be mentored by Sir Ken Robinson, Dr. Steve Peary, or Geoffrey Canada. As a ministry leader I would love to be mentored by A.R. Bernard or Andy Stanley. Sure, I can read their books, watch their videos, or attend their presentations, but because these individuals are so notable in their disciplines, there will always be distance between us.

Dr. Chand suggests that one of the biggest mistakes we make today when choosing a mentor is going after someone who is way ahead of us instead of looking to connect with someone who is just slightly ahead of us.

Think of it this way: if you've just started teaching it probably makes more sense to look for mentor in someone who has 3 to 5 years of experience versus someone with 20 years of experience. Similarly, if you're pastoring 100 people, maybe you should look at finding a mentor who pastors 250 people, instead of 1,200 people. The idea is that you can learn a lot from people who are emerging that may have more instant application to your current position than someone more established. If you currently have a mentor who is several steps ahead of you, consider supplementing that relationship by connecting with someone who is just slightly ahead of you.

If you want to lead well you'll have in your square someone who can mentor you.

Mentoring Someone

My youngest daughter Ella is preparing for kindergarten. It's amazing to watch a young child experiencing this milestone. She is full of questions, concerns, fears and excitement. I tried to explain to her that I've been there before, but in her mind, I'm too far ahead. It's hard to imagine her dad being in elementary school. There is one person my youngest daughter never fails to listen to and that's her big sister, Briana. I have overheard Briana, a second grader, answering Ella's questions about the first day of school. Briana shared her insights about teachers, lunchtime, recess, and making friends. What's really happening is that my oldest daughter is mentoring my youngest daughter on how to navigate through life as a kindergartner, and she's doing it proudly.

Part of your growth as a leader will come from mentoring someone else. There will always be someone who is currently experiencing a stage that you have already navigated through, the more you give advice and counsel other, the more you grow confident in your leadership. If you're not mentoring someone else, you're missing out of one of your greatest opportunities to grow and learn.

If you want to lead well you'll have someone in your square that you are mentoring.

Connecting With Peers

If mentors are slightly ahead, and if those who you are mentoring you are slightly behind, then peers are those who are in step with you. They may be people who work in the same area, attend the same training program, or are part of the same social organization. Connecting to peers can have a reciprocal mentoring feel to it.

When I used to teach college speech courses I enjoyed critiquing speeches during the first half of the semester. I would critique each speech and prepare students for the next presentations. In the second half of the semester I always switched to a more enjoyable strategy. I would not critique any speeches. Instead, I trained the students to critique each other.

Students found the critiques from their peers easier to process than those given by me. The comments weren't coming from someone with years of experience giving and analyzing speeches. The comments were coming from someone who was in the same boat that they were in. It's worth thinking about: who's in the same boat that you're in? How could you benefit from connecting with them?

If you want to lead well you'll strong peers in your square.

Being Supported

The theme song in the movie Toy Story is "You Got a Friend in Me" by Randy Newman. The song echoes the sentiments expressed by two of the main characters in the movie, a toy named Woody and his human owner, Andy. The adventures of Woody and Andy solidified their friendship over the years. Then suddenly, the arrival of a new toy, a space ranger named Buzz Lightyear, changes the dynamics of their relationship. For Woody and Buzz the adventure of being separated from Andy and then reunited with him later in the movie solidified their friendship.

We all need friends that will go on adventures with us.

We need friends that will challenge us. We need friends that will stick with us no matter what happens. We need friends who are not enamored by our positions or accolades. You could be broke or billionaire. You could be famous or inconspicuous. You could be a picture of health or of infirmity. No matter what, your good friends will be there.

As a leader you need a close group of friends. I am fortunate enough to have some friends who have stuck with me through every major phase of my life. Our adventures together have solidified our friendship. They have walked beside me when I was struggling to find my purpose and fighting with insecurities. My friends have been there through my failures and successes. They have been vital to my leadership.

If you want to lead well you'll have good friends in your square.

The Wrap Up

There's protection for leaders inside of a The Leader's Square. If properly nurtured the relationships in the leader square will be a tremendous asset on your journey as an emerging leader.

Keys Questions To Ripening Well:

Do you have all the key relationships that make up the leader square? If not which ones do you need to develop? Take some time intentionally to thank those who are a part of your square.

Lesson 7: The Opportunity of a Lifetime

What if tomorrow an email landed in your inbox and presented the opportunity of a lifetime? What if you were given a chance to lead a project, initiative, or team that would have far reaching implications? What if your work had the potential to positively affect thousands of people for years to come? Would you take it or would you convince yourself that you weren't ripe enough?

I know what Sir Richard Branson would do. He went from dropping out of high school to becoming one of the world's most influential entrepreneurs. Branson's Virgin Group owns and operates hundreds of companies around the globe. The consummate risk taker and chance taker has kite surfed across the English Channel, hasn't met a hot air balloon he didn't love, and holds a world record for being the fastest to cross the Atlantic Ocean in a speedboat. If that wasn't enough Branson's team is also working on a project to make access to space travel just as easy taking a flight on Virgin America Airlines.

Here's what Branson says about those once in a lifetime opportunities, "if somebody offers you an amazing opportunity but you are not sure you can do it, say yes – then learn how to do it later!" Starting out, I'm sure Branson didn't know how to operate an international conglomerate but definitely learned how to do it along the way. Amazing things can happen when you're willing to take a chance.

I'm not sure if Michael Rao knows Richard Branson but I think he would agree with Branson's advice.

Michael Rao Took the Chance

What if your once in a lifetime opportunity was to serve as a college president before your thirtieth birthday? In the mid-90s, Mission College in Santa Clara, California selected Dr. Michael Rao to serve as president. At the time, this made him the youngest college president in the country. He was 28-years-old. This was remarkable, especially considering the report from the American Council of Education that the average age of a college president was 52. What was a life like for a chief administrator this young? I had an opportunity to connect with Dr. Rao and ask him about his experience. Here's what he had to share:

Pierre Quinn: In your late 20s, Mission College trusted you with the office of the president. For a time, you were the youngest college president in the nation. What was that experience like?

Michael Rao: I had no fears. I was like a young kid on a ski slope: the faster I went, the less I feared anything. I'm not sure that I really understood the risks and liabilities, and that propelled my creativity and ability to engage with people. It was an exciting time because I was so young; I'd work 80-hour weeks and still couldn't wait to get started again the next week.

My faculty colleagues were clearly behind my hiring. They were so cooperative and supportive. I had everyone on my side. We really were focusing at that time on building a strategic plan centered on higher academic standards. We were also an underbuilt campus, and so we needed to finish that. In the end, we wanted our reputation to be as Silicon Valley's premier college, because we had really been fueled by the growth going on the Silicon Valley at that time.

I think being this couldn't have happened anywhere but Silicon Valley, where the mindset was that people didn't trust anyone over 30. A presidency like mine wouldn't have happened in any other place. But I gave them every second that I had, and I enjoyed it.

PQ: Before you became president of Mission College, you served as an assistant to the president, a dean, and ran your own consulting firm. How did those experiences help prep you to be a president?

MR: All of that was very helpful. In all of those roles, I spent a lot of times watching other leaders be effective and ineffective, and that helped me define my style and who I am as a leader. There's no question about that.

PQ: How did you navigate working with faculty and administrators who, in many cases, were much older than you?

MR: They were really behind me and supportive in full force. People were very embracing and really very nice. The staff too. I think some of the administrators saw my creative approaches as naïve, and they were less willing to take risks than I was. But that taught me the importance of quickly shaping and developing my own team.

PQ: Age is often a big factor when considering someone for a senior leadership role. What would you say to the young adult who feels their age is a disadvantage in their field?

MR: I'm someone who grew up around older people my entire life. And I learned from them that emotional maturity and thoughtfulness are what matter. There's a great ability to benefit from the wisdom of those who are your senior in age. Listen, and get their advice.

PQ: What was one of your biggest leadership blunders while serving at Mission College?

MR: My tendency toward attending to details, which distracted me from more strategic things. For example, I would read all of the mail that came in, because that's what I thought you were supposed to do. I didn't delegate enough. But that's something I learned to do better as I gained more experience.

PQ: If you could go back and give advice to your 28-year-old self, what would you say?

MR: Be more strategic and focused. Don't worry about listening to everyone and trying to make everyone happy. Remember that it's a marathon, not a sprint. And constantly keep the mission in mind, because it's the mission that ultimately matters, not the business.

What is Michael Rao doing now?

After his time at Mission College Dr. Rao went on to serve as the chancellor of Montana State University and the President of Central Michigan University. Today Dr. Rao serves as the President of Virginia Commonwealth University (VCU) and the Virginia Commonwealth Health System in Richmond, Virginia. In his work he serves the over 30,000 students, 3000+ part time and full time faculty, and over 21,000 employees at VCU and the VCU Medical Center.

The Wrap Up

Eventually someone is going to offer you the opportunity of a lifetime. You can either take the offer and learn along the way or let the opportunity pass and wrestle with the nagging thought "what would have happened if".

Keys Questions To Ripening Well:

1. If someone offered you the opportunity of a lifetime what would make you hesitant to accept it?

2. Dr. Rao described the impact that watching other leaders had on his own ability to lead. Make a list of 3 effective and 3 ineffective leaders that you've worked with. Describe what makes them effective or ineffective. As you consider your own leadership what qualities or behaviors are contributing to your effectiveness? What about your ineffectiveness?

3. What were some other insights that you gained from the interview with Dr. Rao?

Lesson 8: How To Win Over Most Of Your Critics

Ever wish your detractors would just go away?

A critic is someone who expresses an unfavorable opinion of something. We face critics in every area of life. They're not going anywhere. Since we're stuck with them, maybe there's a way you can win over most of them (you'll never win over all of them, so don't even try).

If you're a filmmaker, John Truby can teach you how to win over your critics. Truby is a legendary writer, story coach, and consultant. For decades Truby taught writers, directors, and producers the keys to good filmmaking. Some of Truby's students have gone on to create several critically acclaimed films. Over 30,000 people around the world have taken his script-writing course.

Keys to Winning Over Film Critics

For filmmakers, the key to success is making a great movie, not focusing on your critics. Truby offers several elements of a great movie. He considers the following three to be essential:

1. A central character with the goal, problem, or idea.

Great movies feature strong central characters. These characters either have a goal, a problem to solve, or an idea that can change the world. You won't have a good movie without a strong central character.

2. Causing the audience to believe in the main characters cause.

The cause of the central character has to resonate with the audience. The cause can be a quest for love, a search for meaning, a journey for resolution, or a desire for connection. Great moviemakers work to create a movie that makes you cheer for the central character.

3. Room to breathe

Great stories that become great movies need room to breathe. Twists and turns are a must. Every scene isn't about the main character, but each scene impacts the perspective the audience has on the movie's main idea.

Over the years many green directors, producers, and screenwriters have risen to international prominence because of their understanding of these key elements. They gained raving reviews from critics by not focusing on the critics but by focusing on the goal - making a great movie.

Keys To Winning Over Critics of Your Leadership

Leadership expert John Maxwell tells a story from his early days as a pastor. On a church wide evaluation most the members of the small church gave him a high approval rating. However, there were a few people who didn't feel like he was a good fit for the church. When speaking to his father about this, Maxwell shared that he wanted to find out the names of the few who didn't approve of him.

His father told him to only have a handful of people disapprove of you is probably the best leadership rating that you'll get in your entire life. You will never be able to win over everyone who criticizes you. Our focus shouldn't be on making everyone happy. So here are four principles that can help you win over most of your critics (without focusing on them):

1. Consistency

Don't start anything you can't sustain. As a leader, you might have tons of great ideas, but you shouldn't try to implement every one. You should focus on doing a few things well. In his book Essentialism: The Disciplined Pursuit of Less, Greg McKeown suggests that one of the biggest mistakes that leaders make is that we allow ourselves to be pulled in multiple directions making minimal progress in each direction. McKeown tells leaders to focus on the one or two things that can have the most impact and remove everything else that isn't essential.

Think back to Lesson 5 and our discussion about the leader's pace. Remember why the tortoise won? The key was keeping a consistent pace. I once worked with a leader who was big on starting things with high fanfare and excitement, every initiative started over the top, every program began with a flair, every event was a primetime production. The challenge with making everything grand is that you create a culture that demands that all things be grand, all the time. This is not sustainable. When the excitement of the new project dissipates, the remedy for this type of leader is to simply start something else. Consistency is about producing your work at your determined level of excellence and doing so regularly.

Don't waste time attempting to be great at everything every once in a while. Be great at your one thing consistently.

2. Quality

One of the frequently asked questions on the Rolls Royce website is how long does it take to go from order to delivery when ordering a new Rolls Royce?

Here's how they answer:

Every Rolls-Royce motorcar is painstakingly hand-built and hand-finished to exceptionally high standards. This exacting approach distinguishes Rolls Royce from other manufacturers but it also takes time.

The point is: people are willing to wait for quality.

That is probably why there are long lines for new (Michael) Jordan sneakers, the latest iPhone, and for that hole in the wall restaurant that serves great food.

If consistency is repeatable action then quality is doing those repeatable actions with excellence.

Have you put on a new pair of pants and discovered a small round sticker in the pocket? It will say inspected by number 18 or some other number. The better the quality of the garment the lower the inspection number.

There is a big difference between a pair of jeans that has been inspected by number 95 and a pair Jeans that has been inspected by number 5. If your work as a leader were to be given a quality inspection how would it be rated?

3. Dependability

Dependability is rooted in reliability and trust. Trust is developed over time. Sure you might have consistency and sure you may have quality but dependability comes down to answering the question in the hearts of those you lead. When they need help, when they need support, when they need assistance, are you available? Additionally, people often want to know if you will face the challenges when things become difficult or if you will run away.

4. Teachability

You can learn something from everyone. Everyone has different experiences, backgrounds, and perspectives. A good leader is in a constant state of learning. As teams of people change, technology advances, and operations improve, leaders must be teachable. The moment you feel you've learned everything and believe there is nothing else to learn, you cease to serve and you limit your ability to lead effectively. Scheduling learning conversations at every level of your organization helps you to be a better leader.

Everyone, from the president's office to the janitor's closet, has knowledge to offer. Consider arranging conversations with individuals you would not normally come in contact with. Lunch is a great time to do it.

When you sit down ask them what they think about a certain initiative project or play. Ask them what their experiences have been working with the company and observe how the respond to various questions and concerns. There's always more you can learn about your industry; there's always more you can learn about the people you lead; there's always more you can learn about those you're looking to serve; there's always more you can learn about the areas you want to have impact on; and there's always more you can learn about yourself.

Henry Doherty, the founder of CITGO once said, “Be a student as long as you still have something to learn and this will mean all of your life.”

The Wrap Up

The key to winning over those critical to your leadership is to not spend your time focusing on them but to spend your time focusing on doing good work.

Keys To Ripening Well:

1. Select a few people both inside and outside your organization to rate your consistency, quality, dependability, and teachability as a leader. Use this feedback to develop an action plan for working on these areas.

2. Schedule lunch and learning meetings with different people in your organization for the next month. Ask them key questions about the organization, their experience, and their perspective on a major plan, project or idea.

3. Winston Churchill once said, "Criticism may not be agreeable, but it is necessary. It fulfills the same function as pain in the human body. It calls attention to an unhealthy state of things." Have a conversation with one of the most outspoken critics of your leadership. Spend most of the time listening and taking notes. After the conversation, review the valid points the person made.

Lesson 9: The Benefits of Getting Things Wrong

Diana Laufenberg likes it when her students make mistakes.

Laufenberg has been an educator for nearly 20 years. She has taught social studies, geography, and various government courses. Currently, she serves as the Managing Director and lead teacher of Inquiry Schools in Philadelphia, a school designed to challenge the way the students traditionally learn.

In 2010, Laufenberg was invited to put on a Ted Talk on the importance of making mistakes. In the talk, she suggests that, in a properly facilitated environment, mistakes are key to students' success. She believes that we live in a world with unlimited access to information and that learning to apply that information is a messy process. She instructs us, "to tell kids to never be wrong to ask them to always have the right answer doesn't allow them to learn." For Laufenberg, failure is one of the best instructional methods. In order for you to ripen well as a leader you have to embrace making mistakes. The question is when you will make your next mistake, not if.

Why do mistakes happen?

Mistakes fall into three major categories: lack of information, lack of training, and lack of energy. Let's test this theory. When you think about your last mistake does it fall into one of these three categories? I'm sure it does.

Considered by many to be the grandfather of public speaking Dale Carnegie says, 'the successful man will profit from his mistakes and try again in a different way" Legendary UCLA basketball coach John Wooden says, "if you're not making mistakes you're not doing anything."

After making a few mistake analysis paralysis you may start to develop analysis paralysis. Analysis paralysis is a condition where you analyze a situation for so long until finally apprehension settles in and you don't make any decision at all. My oldest daughter Briana used to suffer from analysis paralysis. Her goal is to be a master artist. She is meticulous when she colors, draws, or paints. Her face lights up when she engaged in art projects, until she makes a mistake. When she used to make mistakes frustration would grab her and the end result would be a balled up piece of paper taking its final rest in the trashcan. “I don’t want to be an artist anymore,” she would declare.

Several years ago we took a trip to New York and visited the Museum of Natural History. Coming down to the end of our tour, we noticed a group of art students gathered around their professor. They were receiving instructions about their assignment for the day. I watched as the professor explained to his pupils what he wanted them to focus on. They clutched their drawing pads with rapt attention. As the students were dismissed I made my way to the professor an introduced Briana, who was hiding shyly behind me. I shared with the professor some insights into Briana’s artistic journey.

For a few moments the professor took some time to encourage Briana to continue to work on her craft. I asked the professor about artists and making mistakes. I told him that Briana has a tough time making mistakes. Turning to Briana he smiled and said, "You should make mistakes all the time as an artist, because that's the only way you can learn. It's the only way that you’re going to grow."

I know you want to ripen into an effective leader, but how comfortable are you with making mistakes? Here are a few of the major mistakes I’ve made as a leader.

Not Finishing the Task

The summer after high school I worked in a fudge shop at the mall. We did more than make fudge, we created productions. The fudge was made out in the open and we had to sing and dance through the process. The singing and dancing drew a crowd that we would then persuade to buy the fresh fudge. It was a fun job.

Eventually, I was given the opportunity to become a manager in training. For a high school graduate transitioning to college, the idea of a manager in training was a big deal for me. The responsibilities of manager in training included coordinating the work schedule, the fudge production schedule, and addressing customer complaints. The most important part of the job was making the daily deposit. At the midpoint of the day, the manager on duty would count down the cash registers and drop the funds at the bank located in the mall.

On this particular day we were very busy. The scheduled time to make the deposit was getting close but there was quite a bit of activity in the store. I was headed out of the store to make the deposit when a few of the staff asked for my help. Instead of placing the funds in the store safe until I could make the deposit I stuck them in what I thought was a safe place. I know what you're thinking: why on earth would you do that? Well, it was something I'd watched my manager do a few times before when he had to handle an issue before heading to the bank.

The activity of the rest of my shift caused me to completely forget the deposit. I went through the rest of my day, finished my shift, and went home. A couple of hours later I received a phone call from the afternoon manager asking for the paper verifying the deposit. A shuddered when I remember the "safe" place. I told him where to find the funds and feeling of devastation came over me when he responded that the money was gone.

Here's the painful lesson I learned that day: as a leader, I need to finish the tasks at hand.

Not Fostering Relationships

Another major leadership mistake I made when was early in my pastoral career. I arrived at a small church in Kentucky full of life, ideas, and plans for the church I'd developed in seminary. A few weeks into my tenure I began to outline what was to be my vision for the church. I was preaching sermons, I was teaching classes, and I was trying to motivate church members to get around this great vision for the church. Very few of the people in the church were willing to buy into the vision. They didn't know me. It's hard for people to trust it's hard for people to trust or follow someone they didn't know. I was expecting movement without relationship.

If you're not building relationships, it doesn't matter how grand your vision is, people aren't going to come on board. The major lesson I learned from that experience was that building relationships is just as important than casting vision.

Not Valuing Someone's Opinion

When my wife and I got married she drove an old Ford Windstar and I drove an old Buick LeSabre. I gave the Buick away to a friend who really needed a car and we learned to share the Windstar. Like all old vehicles the Windstar started to give us trouble. As two newlywed college kids we were devastated to hear the mechanic give us a $1,000 estimate for a repair.

After begging and borrowing we were able to scrape up with the money. Then I had a bright idea. Why not take the $1,000 make a down payment on a better car. My wife adamantly expressed her desire to take the money to repair the van. As the leader of our home I made the final decision to move ahead with the purchase of a car. My reasoning was that I was the man of the house and knew more about cars than she did. I never said it was good reasoning, just my reasoning. This new car ended up being more trouble than it was worth. For years I asked myself what life would have been like has I valued the opinion of my wife and repaired the van.

I know what you're thinking the lesson that I'm going to share is "listen to your wife." Let's put it a differently. As a leader you must learn to value the input of those you are leading. They very well might have a better solution to a problem than you do.

The Wrap Up

We've all made mistakes by not finishing tasks, fostering relationships, or valuing the input of others. Growth happens when we take the opportunity to learn from those mistakes.

Keys Questions To Ripening Well:

1. What's one of the mistakes you've made growing up? What did you learn from the experience?

2. When was the last time that fear of making a mistake caused you to delay or neglect making a vital leadership decision?

3. Do you feel that leaders should always get things right or should they have the latitude to make mistakes?

Lesson 10: Taking Notes On The Journey

How much would you pay to have one conversation with one of the most influential people in history?

Now what if this influential person was Leonardo da Vinci, the artist who painted the Mona Lisa and the Last Supper? How much would this conversation be worth to you? Would you pay $1,000, $10,000, $100,000, or $1,000,000?

For Bill Gates, the founder of Microsoft, a conversation with Da Vinci was worth over $30,000,000 to him..

In 1994, Gates purchased one of the 30 remaining journals belonging to Leonardo da Vinci. This 72-page diary contains the thoughts and sketches of da Vinci. The Guardian newspaper regards a look inside one of these journals as a "fascinating insight into his mind." One of journals, named Codex Arundel, has been digitized by the British Library and uploaded to the Internet. Now anyone can virtually a peek inside of da Vinci's mind. Reading da Vinci's journal would almost be like having a conversation with him.

For Bill Gates, 30-million is a cheap price to pay to experience the journey of the man who became one of history's most influential artists, mathematicians, and engineers. Years ago, Da Vinci probably had no idea that the ramblings in his notebooks would be worth so much.

A not so secret urge of every little boy is to get his hands on his sister's diary. A slap, a punch, a kick, a bite or scream is a small price to pay for insights into her mind. David Sedaris says, "If you read someone else's diary, you get what you deserve." A peek inside of your sister's diary is like a fascinating insight into her mind.

For a number of years I've kept various journals handy. They've become a collection of thoughts from the day, presentation notes, dreams, and challenges. I've also included late-night brainstorms, advice from my mentor, and mistakes I've made. Much of this book finds its origin in those journals. In this way, you would benefit greatly from keeping a journal.

Journal For Legacy

Keeping a journal gives you an opportunity to leave a legacy.

King Solomon, the wisest man who ever lived, hits us with this sobering reality: "whatever you find to do whatever you find to do with your hands do with all your might because there is neither work nor planning nor knowledge nor wisdom in the grave; the place where you'll eventually go." Solomon reminds us that everybody has his or her appointment with death and once you reach the point of death there is no one last thing. You won't be able to share one last insight. There won't be any opportunities to have one last conversation.

Years after you're gone people will be thumbing through old pictures of you asking what you were like and what was life like for you. Journaling will allow your thoughts and passion to live on for years to come. Over the years scores of people have gleaned insights from Martin Luther King Jr.'s diary from jail, Nelson Mandela's prison diary, Harry Truman's presidential diary, and General Patton's war diary. Their writings constitute a large part of their legacy. Today they still allow us to peek inside of their minds.

Journal for Learning

Several years ago a friend quoted one of his college professors that still rings true: “people forget, paper remembers”. The idea is that there's a likelihood you'll forget the most important things if you don't record them. British journalist Bill Self puts it this way, “always carry a notebook. And I mean always. The short-term memory only retains information for three minutes; unless it is committed to paper you can lose an idea for ever.”

Harvard Business School professor, Teresa Amberly, offers that journaling is one of the best productivity tools that we have. More than the apps, more than the programs, more than the classes on productivity, the best way to increase productivity is to keep a journal.

Have you ever heard someone refer to an expert as someone who has forgotten more about a subject than you could ever learn? I'm sure that might be a testimony to their intellect and to research habits, but it's also a sad indictment. It's sad that the amount of things that they've learned over the years has been lost because they weren't recorded. Keeping a journal is one of the best things a leader can do and here are a few ways to do it.

The Old-Fashioned Notebook

Head down to your nearest office supply store and grab a composition book, a spiral notebook or legal pad. If you want to get fancy you can even go to the bookstore and have your mind blown with a number of journal options out there. You can even purchase handcrafted specially designed journals online that are tailored to meet your specifications.

The Digital Journal

Microsoft Word or another word processing program or even Google Docs is another way that people like to journal. They simply open up a Google doc or blank Microsoft Word document, at the end of every day or the beginning of every morning and take notes. There's also a great app called Evernote. Evernote is a note-taking app, which will allow you to record notes on your digital devices. One of the benefits of Evernote is that is sync across all your digital devices. Whatever I type on my iPhone is automatically synced to my iPad and MacBook.

A Blog

The term blog is short for weblog. A blog is a website on which someone writes about personal opinions, activities, and experiences. When I first started blogging my intention was to record my life journey. Many of the most popular blogs that are followed are followed because people are transparent about their journey and share their resources. A simple Google search on how to start a blog is a good place to begin.

A Vlog

A vlog is much like a blog but instead the posts are in video form. Video content is very popular today and some people have built thriving businesses around it. Consider setting up a YouTube channel where you record insights from lessons you've learned, things that you've experienced, or even your week in review. Some of the most popular YouTube channels are from business leaders and entrepreneurs sharing their story providing some insights or answering questions from their journey.

The Wrap Up

Whatever method you choose, keeping notes of your experience is a good way to learn and grow as a leader. The notes that you take will benefit you and others for years to come but you have to select a way to record your insights so that they will be remembered.

Keys Questions To Ripening Well:

1. Which of the journal methods are you interested in using or are you already using?

2. Schedule a time to consistent time to journal. If you're a blogger or vlogger email me (picrre@pierrecquinn.com) a link to your latest journal entry.

Lesson 11: Team Leadership For Green Leaders

I was late for my first leadership team meeting.

We all hate the feeling of walking into a room where everyone is waiting on you. I could read from the facial expressions that they were thinking not only is our pastor young but he's late. Mistakes like that don't produce high confidence rating. It took about a month or two to recover from being late to that first meeting. In Lesson 8 we talked about consistency as one of the keys to winning over your critics. Consistently arriving on time for meetings is a good way to demonstrate this.

In addition to punctuality here are nine other tips to help you better lead a team:

Tip 1: Know Yourself

What's your temperament?

What's your personality type?

What are your greatest strengths?

What are your greatest challenges?

What are your passions? What are your interests?

What are your fears?

Leading well requires awareness and acceptance and an appreciation of you. You cannot confidently lead others without a continual journey of self-discovery. A good way to track your journey of self-discovery would be to record it in your journal (see lesson 10).

Tip 2: Play to Your Strengths. Recruit Your Weaknesses.

Years ago I took the Clifton Strengths Finder assessment. According to www.gallupstrengthscenter.com over 12 million people around the world have taken this assessment. Developed by Donald Clifton and Tom Rath, the assessment helps individuals to identify their top 5 strengths out of a possible 34 options.

My top five strengths are:

- Ideation
- Connectedness
- Learner
- Communication
- Input

When you look at my unique combination of strengths, they lend themselves to strategic thinking, and big picture planning, but they also come with their own set of weaknesses. Two of my weaknesses are lack of attention to details and struggling with execution. As a dreamer and big picture thinker I would do well to connect with someone who is highly detail oriented and highly skilled at execution. But if I don't know my strengths I can't partner with others who can work in the areas where I am weak. If you don't know your strengths, how can you play to them? By learning your strengths and accepting your weaknesses you will be willing to partner with people who are strong in areas that you are not.

Tip 3: Reaffirm The Value of Your Team

Even if you never studied Maslow's hierarchy of needs, you've experienced it in your life.

According to Abraham Maslow's research our needs fall into a hierarchy. The most basic needs are physiological, food, clothing ,and shelter. When that need is met we can move on to the idea of safety and security. Safety and security refers to being in safe place physically and emotionally. The next step up on Maslow's hierarchy is this idea of love and belonging. We all have a need to be connected to other people. Next comes self-esteem. This refers to the ability to see yourself and a person of value. Maslow lists our final need as self-actualization. This is the ability to realize and work toward your full potential.

In a professional setting where people are working in a way that allows them to meet their physiological (food and clothing) and safety needs (a place to live), it becomes more than just a job. The next step in the hierarchy is satiating that need to belong. People want to feel like they belong. In this area your challenge as a leader is to remind your team, both individually and collectively, of their personal value and their contribution to the overall organization.

One of the things that I did to reaffirm the value of a group that I was working with was to change the function and identity of the group from a church board to a church leadership team.

Let's look at the definitions for each:

- Board: a group of people constituted as the decision-making body of an organization
- Leadership Team: a group of people who make important decisions and lead initiatives that

help an organization reach particular goals or objectives

A church board can connote the idea of making decisions from a distance. This definition of leadership team suggests not just making decisions but being hands on in the implementation of those decisions. A team makes decisions and leads the charge to carrying out of those decisions is significantly more valuable than a team that doesn't.

Tip 4: Challenge Privately but Acknowledge Openly

On one occasion I worked with a team member who was not satisfied with my leadership. He made several comments to others that were quite toxic. In my frustration I wanted to challenge him openly but knew that wasn't the best course of action. Instead we had a face-to-face meeting.

In the meeting I asked for his opinion about my leadership and about the statements I'd heard. It wasn't an easy conversation but it was a needed one. I challenged him to be a better support to the team. I also asked him to share any concerns about my leadership with me before he shared them with someone else. After challenging him privately I openly acknowledge him for his hard work, commitment, and support of the organization. Over time I gained the support of others in the organization in spite of this person's comments.

Note: There will be times when you will have to openly challenge those who are opposed to your leadership. Choose those times very wisely.

Be More Captain Than Coach

In 2004, the NBA finals pitted the Los Angeles Lakers against the Detroit Pistons. The Lakers embodied showtime and flare. The Detroit Pistons, a team built on journeymen basketball players. They embodied the hard-working blue-collar spirit of Detroit and were led by Hall of Fame coach Larry Brown. The Pistons defeated the Lakers in 5 games.

Coach Brown had an intense love for the game and an insight that found few rivals but Coach Brown never played one games in the 2004 NBA Finals. He only coached the players. Often during intense moments Coach Brown would call a play but it was up to the leader of the team to execute. The leader on the floor was the Pistons' point guard and captain, Chauncey Billups. Billups took the mission of the organization and not only kept it from the team but he also was instrumental in helping the team to fulfill that mission. Billups was named the Most Valuable Player of the 2004 NBA Final because of his leadership on the basketball court. When the game is on line the people you're leading need a captain more than they need a coach.

Tip 5: Delegate Then Empower

Delegate

ˈdeləˌgāt/

verb
entrust (a task or responsibility) to another person, typically one who is less senior than oneself

Empower

əmˈpou(ə)r/

verb

give (someone) the authority or power to do something

Chances are you might be doing a little too much.

How many roles are you doing in your current position? How many of roles things are things that only you can do? How many of those things are things that others can be empowered to do?

Stop trying to do everything.

Most leaders get in trouble because they take on too many things that they can do but shouldn't do. Just because you can do something doesn't mean that you should.

Identify the tasks in your organization that only you can do and should do. For everything else find people in your organization to empower and delegate those responsibilities to them. By empowering and delegating responsibilities to others you are actually working to develop more leaders in your organization.

Tip 6: Keep Casting the Vision

In his book Making Vision Stick, Andy Stanley suggests that casting vision is not something that happens just once a year or once a quarter. The vision of the organization needs to always be before the people and we need to continue to remind them of what that vision is. In fact, you should filter everything the organization does through the lens of the vision. Every organization has the potential to hit a rut and in the rut then the question starts.

What the point?

What's it all for?

Who cares?

That's why it's important for leaders to keep the vision in front of the people.

After you cast the vision for your organization cast it again, and again, and again.

Master the Art of Facilitating Discussions

Talking is easy but connecting takes work.

When you're having a team meeting there are 3 types of people: people who always have something to say, people who have nothing to say, and those who have a difficult time trying to figure out when they should say something or be quiet. Practice getting the most out of your team discussions by creating a space where everyone can contribute and no one person dominate the conversation. That may mean calling on specific people during the course of the discussion and cutting the comments of others.

Help Get the Right People in the Right Place

This is one of the challenges of leading volunteer organizations. As you lead in this space you may be scrambling just to get warm bodies to help. Even in this context you can work to get the right people in the right place.

Take time to review the strengths and weaknesses of each team member. This is just as important as knowing your strengths and weaknesses as a leader. Take a look at the abilities need in each area compared to the abilities of your team. Is each member in the best position to be effective? Reviewing this question may lead to some difficult conversation as you seek to move people to the area that is best of both them and the organization.

The Wrap Up

At 19 years old Sidney Crosby became the captain of the Pittsburg Penguins a professional hockey team in the National Hockey League. He was given the change of a lifetime to lead a team who has some members twice his age. Crosby excelled in the role proving that young leaders can lead great teams.

Key Questions To Ripening Well:

1. Which of the nine areas of team leadership are the most difficult for you?

2. Review your notes on The Leader's Square in Lesson 5. Which of those who make up your square can help you with the challenges that you listed in question number 1?

Lesson 12: Learning To Hang On

The McNaughton Company doesn't make the only banana hook sold on Amazon.com but it does make one of the most reviewed ones. Weighing in at three tenths of an ounce and measuring at five inches the banana hook isn't much to look at. The design is simple yet hundreds of people have declared its awesome effectiveness. Over 400 people have reviewed The McNaughton Banana Hook and the large majority of those reviews are being four or five stars.

Here's the product description as listed on Amazon:

- Mounts under a cabinet.
- Holds a bunch of bananas.
- Folds out of sight when not in use.

The success of this product and others like is built on the theory that bananas ripen better when they have something to hang onto. Here are four resources that if held on to could help you to ripen well.

Hold on to Good Reading

The library in Independence, Missouri had approximately 1,700 books during the late 1800s and early 1900s. Former President Harry Truman once claimed to have read all the books in the library in his town growing up. While no one has verified the accuracy of Truman's assertion no one can deny the impact that reading had on his life. "Not all readers are leaders, but all leaders are readers," Truman said.

One of the richest men in the world, Warren Buffet, once shared one of the secrets to his success. When asked about how to get smarter Buffet held up a stack of papers and said, "read 500 pages like this every day. That's how knowledge builds up, like compound interest."

A 2013 Huffington post poll suggested that 28% of people living in the United States had not read an entire book in the previous year. I wonder how many of those were serving in a leadership capacity?

If you want to lead well, you need to read.

If you want to lead smarter, you need to read.

The insights and information gleaned from reading good books both inside and outside of your industry and primary interest are things leaders need to hang onto.

Hold on to Good Training

There's nothing like a good conference, workshop, or training program I call these sorts of things "learning events". To date I've never walked away from a learning event thinking that it was a complete waste of time. There are hundreds and hundreds of conferences and workshops for you to attend. Check both inside and outside your organization to find which learning event best suits your context.

Some of the best organizations in the world stay on top because they retain good leaders. How do they do this? They have created strong leadership development programs.

Here are three good reasons to attend a learning event:

1. Leaders Like You are in the Room

Years ago I served as the annual giving coordinator for my alma mater. Annual giving is the entry-level introduction to fundraising and development in many organizations. I had no idea what to expect. Working for a small private college I had a modest fundraising goal of a half-million dollars. Much of the funds were raised through our annual phonathon program. I was facing two major challenges when I started this position: I knew nothing about fundraising and I knew nothing about managing a phonathon program.

Shortly after starting my boss sent me to a fundraising conference. One of the first workshops I attended was on how to run a successful annual giving program. At the beginning of the session the presenter asked everyone who was new to fundraising or annual giving to stand. More than half of the people in the room stood up. A huge sigh of relief came over me. I was in the room with people who knew exactly what I was going through. By the end of the conference I made several connections and joined a resource group. Whenever I was feeling overwhelmed or frustrated I would pick up the phone or send an email to someone who would understand.

2. Moments For Reflection

When was the last time you took a moment to reflect on your work? When was the last time did you review what Simon Sinek calls "the why" behind your organization? For many leaders moments of true reflection are few and far between. When we do take time to reflect on where we're serving and what we're doing it through the eyes of an insider. Many learning events tailor their offerings to create moments of reflection. Keynote speakers, breakout sessions, and networking events put you in place to take a step back and look at your organization from the outside.

3. Brainstorms and Idea Generation

A creative learning environment always creates a catalyst for ideas. This is quite helpful for leaders because we seem to always be looking for new ideas. The opportunity to see what other leaders are doing in your field will always spark ideas. Innovation expert Gary Hamel suggests that one of the problems in leadership is that we don't bring enough ideas to the table. Author and speaker Catherine DeVyre says, "the most expensive words in business are we've always done it this way."

Each time I've attended a learning event I've always walked away with tons of ideas that help me as a leader. You might not implement every idea but there is bound to be an idea, which sparks an idea, which sparks another idea that will be valuable to you.

Hold on to Good Influencers

Who are the major influencers? Who are the notable leaders in your field? If you work in education, who are the some of the best administrators across the country? If you're in the sports industry who are some of the notable coaches and trainers? If you work with nonprofits who are some of the best executives?

Leading influencers are doing always doing a combination of three things: writing, speaking, and training or creating. To follow their writing signup for updates to from their blogs and websites. To following their speaking see what videos have been uploaded to YouTube. To following their training and creating look into what conferences feature them as a presenter or what resources they've created and distributed. Many influencers give away an incredible amount of information and resources.

Hold on to Doing Good Work

There is absolutely, positively no substitute for this. Like a mentor told me years ago, “I can give you all the advice and support you need, but you have to do the work.” Reading, attending learning events, and keeping track of notable influencers are all great things to do but they cannot replace doing a good job. Actually, you should be leveraging those things to help you do a good job.

One of Darren Hardy’s keys to accomplishing your dream is hard work. In his book The Compound Effect Hardy says, “If we want to succeed we need to recover our grandparents’ work ethic.” My maternal grandparents worked in a garden every year of their adult life. Gardening takes discipline, patience, and dedication. My paternal grandmother was a business owner and even when her health declined she still worked as a seamstress and jewelry maker. She had a will to keep pushing even when things were tough. Most of our grandparents grew up in an age defined by hard work. If you could combine their work ethic with your creativity and access to technology what would that look like?

Just thinking about it makes me smile too.

The Wrap Up

Thanks for reading through Leading While Green. Now that you've spent some time in reflection now is the time for action. Begin to implement some of the key insights you've gained from this book. I look forward to one day hearing the story of how you've ripened well.

Keys Actions To Ripening Well

1. Start a book list of recommended reads. Besides list on Amazon.com or Barnes and Noble check with other leaders you know to see what they're reading. Set goal to read at least one book a month that will help you grow as a leader.

2. Make plans to attend at least one learning event sponsored by your organization and one outside of your organization during the next 6 months. Be sure to network and take notes.

3. Make a list of notable leaders in your field. Select 3 and if they have website/blogs sign-up for the updates and free resources they provide.

4. Write down all of your responsibilities as a leader. Choose one to apply your grandparents' work ethic to (if they had a good one) over the next month. Record the impact of this intentional effort.

About The Author

Pierre Quinn is passionate about helping others live, learn, and lead with confidence. As a speaker, author, and pastor Pierre travels across the country sharing messages of success and hope. He currently resides with his wife and two daughters in South Central Kentucky. You can connect with Pierre on Twitter (@pierrequinn), on Facebook (MrPierreQuinn) or on his blog:

(www.pierrecquinn.com)

Made in the USA
Middletown, DE
03 September 2016